For Jeremiah and Joshua

Printed in the United States of America
Keen Vision Publishing, LLC
www.publishwithKVP.com
ISBN: 978-0-578-90260-9

THE AMAZING ADVENTURES OF US

A TRIP TO THE AQUARIUM

By Laura Daisy

KEEN VISION PUBLISHING

Adventure awaits! It's time to explore!
Let's journey through rivers and oceans and more.

Up, up and away we go,
We must go to the top to voyage below.

River otters that swim
And some fast asleep.
Long bodies and tails
And tiny webbed feet.

Look over here!

Alligators and turtles
Toes painted green, red, yellow and purple.

Let's see something else!

Fish galore.
There are so many fish
We can't count them anymore!
Some with black stripes, some yellow, some blue.
Some swim alone, others travel in schools.

Look over here!

Salamanders, how cool!
You would think they were lizards
But don't you be fooled.
Amphibians they are
Brown bodies and yellow spots
Shiny, wet skin, dry they are not.

Mossy frogs hard to see
Their skin blends with the trees.
How clever they are, so hidden within
Can you find them all? In total, there's 10.

Hello, penguin family
Nice to meet you, indeed.
Would you waddle for me?
Will you show me your wings?

We can touch something here!

Mr. Sturgeon, is that you?
They feel very weird but also so cool!

Look over here!

Sea turtles so huge!
Much faster in water
They swim and they cruise.

We can touch something here!

Is that you, Ms. Stingray?
She swims to the top!
She wants to play!

One shark! Two sharks!
My, what a sight!
Look at those teeth
We hope they don't bite.

Mr. Lemur so shy, in his tree he sits high.
We dare not bother him, so we bid him goodbye.

Butterfly garden is a beautiful space.
Filled with flowers and trees all over the place
Some fly high and some very low
They glide past our face and tickle our nose.

Look at the jellyfish, see how they flow
And when it is dark, oh how they glow
Watch out in the ocean, don't get caught in between
If you touch a jellyfish, it is sure to sting.

Spider crab, octopus, starfish and a squid
All busy napping.
Shh, shh… quiet kids.

One final stop,
Grab a token for memories.
Bye-bye aquarium.
We will miss you so dearly.

We had such a blast,
An adventure indeed!
Amazing things do happen
When you get out and see.

CPSIA information can be obtained
at www.ICGtesting.com
Printed in the USA
LVHW070304200721
693165LV00002B/50

9 780578 902609